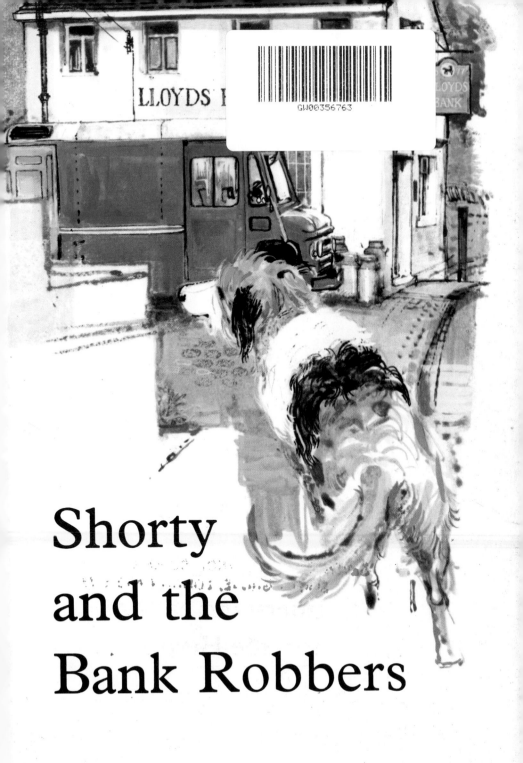

Shorty
and the
Bank Robbers

Thursday is pocket money day.

One Thursday my Dad said, "Who wants pocket money?"

"I do," I said.

Shorty barked.

Shorty the Hero is my best friend.

He cannot talk.

He just barks.

I knew what he meant.

He meant: I do!
I want some pocket money,
too!

My Dad laughed.

He knew what Shorty meant,
too.

"Dogs do not have pocket
money, Shorty," he said.

My Dad felt in his pockets.
"I have no change,"
he said.
"Take this note
to the village bank.
They will be open soon.
They will change it."

So Shorty and I walked
down the road to the bank.

It was a little bank.

Two men worked in it.

Mr Peters and old Mr Jones
worked in the bank.

But the door was shut.

The bank was not open yet.

Shorty and I went round
the yard to the side door.
Mr Peters and Mr Jones
knew Shorty and me.
They would let us in.

The door was open a little.
So we walked in.
I could not see Mr Peters.
I could not see
old Mr Jones.
The bank was empty.
What was going on?

"Wuff!" said Shorty.
He jumped on to the counter.
"Wuff! Wuff!"
I knew what Shorty meant.
Something was wrong.

I ran round the counter.
There was old Mr Jones.
He was tied up!
He was gagged
so that he could not shout.

Then I saw Mr Peters.
He was tied and gagged too.
Something <u>was</u> wrong!
Bundles of money
were all over the floor.
The bank had been robbed!
Shorty barked again.

I ran to old Mr Jones.
"I will soon untie you,"
I said.
I bent down.
But someone grabbed me.
Shorty had barked a warning.
"Help me, Shorty,"
I shouted

Shorty jumped off the counter.
Someone shouted "Ouch!"
Shorty was biting him.
I was free.
I turned round.
    The man Shorty was biting
was very fat.
    He had a mask over his face.
    "Hold him, Shorty," I said.

Then another man ran in.
He had a sack in one hand.
He pulled out a gun.
"Call that dog off," he said.
"Here, Shorty," I said.
What else could I do?
I had to call him off.
Shorty stopped biting.
He came to me.
He thought it was a game.

"Wuff," he said.
"Stop that dog barking,"
said the thin man.
"Tie him up. Gag him."
The fat man grabbed Shorty.

Poor Shorty!
He did not think
it was a game, now.
He struggled and bit.
"Ouch!" said the fat man.
His mask fell off.
I knew him!
He did odd jobs
in the village.
Now he was robbing the bank!
He tied Shorty up.
He gagged him
with a money bag.
Then he said,
"That boy knows me.
We will have to take him
with us."

"We will take his dog, too,"
said the thin man.
"People will think
they have gone for a walk.
Hurry.
The bank should be open
soon."

Then I was tied and gagged.
I was frightened.
Shorty looked frightened,
too.
He struggled,
but he could not move.

19

The fat man filled the sack
with bundles of money.
He got another sack
and bundled Shorty into it.
Poor old Shorty!
The thin man took off
his mask.
I did not know him.

"Come on,"
he said, and picked me up.
He carried me
to the side door.
I tried to struggle,
but I could not move.
I tried to shout,
but I could not make
a sound.

An old van was in the yard.
The back doors were open.
I was pushed inside,
flat on my face.

"Give me a hand,"
said the fat man.

Two sacks landed beside me,
one full of money and
the other full of Shorty.

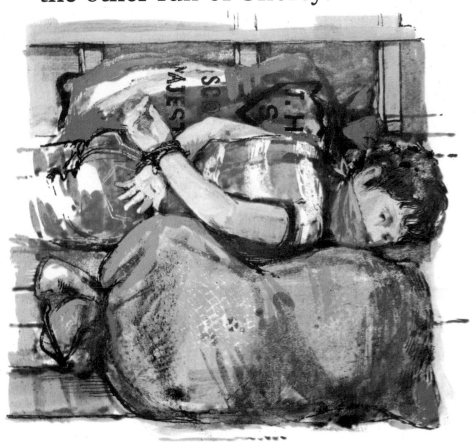

The doors shut.

"Let's get out of here,"
the thin man said.

"What about the boy
and the dog?"
said the other man.

"We will get rid of them
later."

There was a bump.
The van started off.
I was very frightened now.
Shorty and I were in a fix.
I tried to get my hands free.
But I could not.
The men had tied me up
too well.

Shorty tried to get free, too.

I could hear him struggling. But he could not get free.

I wondered what my Dad would think when I did not come home.

Would he think I had gone for a walk with Shorty?

How would he find us?

How would anyone find us?

We were in a real fix.

We went a long way.

Then the van stopped.

The back doors opened.

"Get the dog out," said the thin man.

"We will get rid of him
here."
He took out his gun.
The fat man pulled
Shorty's sack out.
I tried to shout,
"Don't shoot! Please
don't shoot my best friend!"

But I could not.
I was gagged.
Oh, Shorty, I thought,
how can I save you?

Shorty looked out
of the sack.
He looked at the man
with the gun.
He looked back at me.
I thought I saw him wink.

Then he shot out.
He jumped at the thin man.
The gun went flying.
Shorty was off!
How that dog could run!
The thin man picked up
his gun, but Shorty
was out of sight.

He must have got free
inside his sack, I thought.
Now he can fetch help.
What a dog!
What a friend!

The thin man looked at me.
"Your dog has forty miles
to run home," he said.
"And he can't talk.
No one will find us."

The doors shut.
Now I was on my own.
The thin man was right.
Shorty could not help me.
He did not know
where the van was going.
But my best friend
had got away.
I was glad about that.
I rolled over.
Now I could see through
the crack in the doors.
We were going through
a village.
There were men mending
the road.
We had to stop.

Then I saw a policeman
with a motor cycle.

I tried to shout for help,
but I was gagged.

The policeman could not see
me in the van.

Suddenly I saw Shorty.
He came running up the road.
He had followed the van.
He had not gone home!
Hurry, Shorty, I thought.
Hurry, Boy.
Shorty raced up to the back
of the van.

He knew I was inside.
But he could not bark.
He was still gagged
with the money bag.
Shorty caught the bag
on the van bumper.
The gag came off!

He barked and barked
but no one understood.
    Dogs often bark at vans.
    Shorty could not make
anyone understand.
    The van started off.
    I could not see Shorty now.
    We were going faster.

Shorty would not be able to keep up.

His chance to help had gone.

My friend had tried his best, but the policeman had not understood.

We were going faster and faster.

I looked through the crack in the doors.

Suddenly I saw why.

The policeman on a motor cycle was behind us.

Was he following the van?

Did he know something was wrong?

He flashed his light.

He wanted the van to stop.
But the two men
were not going to stop.
The van was rocking
and bumping at speed.
I rocked and bumped too.
I had a job to see out.
Why was the policeman
following? I thought.
He could not see me.

Then I jumped.

The door handle moved
a little.

Through the crack in
the doors, I could just see—
something.

Something on the bumper.

Shorty!

He was holding on to
the handle with his teeth!

That was why the policeman
was following.

Oh Shorty, I thought.

You are a real friend.

A real hero.

The rocking and bumping
got worse.

It was very bad on corners.
One wheel was making
funny noises.
Perhaps we had a flat tyre.

Suddenly the van skidded
right across the road.

I rolled over again.
The sack of money
fell on top of me.
Bundles of notes fell out.
Crash!
Be-bang-CRASH!
The back doors fell open.
We were in the hedge.

There were all sorts
of other noises.
Shouting and barking.
Was Shorty safe?
Was my best friend all right?
I heard a funny sort of bark.
Shorty was saying
he was all right.
He jumped in.

Was I pleased to see him!
He wagged his tail.
He licked my face.

Then he started to bite
the ropes round my arms.
Soon I was free.
What a Hero my friend was!

I gave him a big hug.

"You will have Thursday
pocket money after all,"
I said.

"The bank will give you a reward.
Then you can have bones
every Thursday."

Shorty barked.

He knew what I meant.

Then the policeman looked in.
He saw the money.
He saw the ropes.
His mouth fell open.
"I have handcuffed those men
together," he said.

"But what happened?
What is all this?
Pocket money?"
I told him what had happened.
He sent for a police car
to take the robbers away.
He sent for a car to take
Shorty and me home.

I looked at the van wheel.
The tyre was flat.
That was why the van
had skidded.
That was why the van
had to stop.
Then I saw something funny.
The valve had teeth marks on it.
Someone had been biting it!
Now who had done that?

I looked at Shorty.
Shorty the Hero looked at me.
And this time I am sure
he winked.
Real friends do not need
words to understand each other.
And Shorty the Hero
is a <u>real</u> friend.